Quilt Recipes
By Jen Kingwell
Creative Director

Art Direction, Photography & Book Layout
By Flip Crilley

PUBLISHED 2021
ME & MY GIRLS PTY LTD
87 Beach Road Torquay Vic 3228 Australia
www.jenkingwelldesigns.com
info@jenkingwelldesigns.com

ISBN: 978 - 0 - 645760 - 0 - 4

Copyright © 2021 by Jennifer Kingwell.

All rights reserved. No part of this publication may be reproduced, distributed or transmitted in any form or by any means, without the written permission of ME & MY GIRLS PTY LTD. The patterns in this book are copyrighted and must not be made for resale.

Although every effort has been taken in the preparation of this book. The publisher and author assume no responsibility for errors or omissions. Neither is any liability assumed for damages resulting from use of information contained herein.

FIRST EDITION
PROUDLY PRINTED & BOUND IN AUSTRALIA BY ADAMS PRINT.

Quilt Recipes

For lovers of quilts and baking, a book
that nourishes the soul and the tummy.

BY JEN KINGWELL

There are few designers who really create a niche. Those whose work is developed from their soul and their deep connection with needle and thread, work that is instantly recognizable rather than replicated.

Jen Kingwell is one such designer.

I was invited to teach for Jen at the Amitié Quilt shop well over a decade ago. We had an instant connection with our love of handwork, family and indulging in the sweeter things in life. I remember walking through the doors of Amitié for the first time and being completely overcome with how innovative the space was. It felt fresh and modern yet warm and welcoming. It was brimming with color and pattern and buzzing with delight. It was a place that embraced all makers and creators, and a short time later, I learned why.

Jen was a designer yet, even if the world sang that word in unison, she was far from believing herself as one. The first time I saw Jen's work I was instantly enamored by her creativity, her exceptional way of piecing and style of appliqué. She had this brilliant ability to marry fabrics that others would divorce, pairing quirky fabrics with contemporary, broad stripes with petite plaids, bold patterns with delicate lawns, plus a sprinkling of brights.

This eclectic mix is then snipped and shaped, portioned and separated, masterfully pieced then arranged into a momentous pattern; Patterns that range from geometric to story, patterns that are now generously shared with the world.

Amitié took me back to South Africa, where daily tea time is revered. A delicious slice of something scrumptious with a heavenly cuppa. As quilters, stitchers and makers, we fill our souls with likeminded friendships, feed our souls with hand or machine stitching, and we love to treat ourselves and others to decadent desserts. Jen Kingwell's Quilt Recipes, is a brilliant pairing of captivating pieced projects and delectable desserts. Whether you are a hand or machine piecer, one can relish in each recipe, whether it be a quilt or perhaps something sweet. Enjoy the process of piecing and the challenge of finding, pairing, and arranging diverse patterns and countless colors together, especially those that make you uncomfortable. Savor each kitchen recipe that has been timelessly tested, lovingly passed down and now fondly shared with you, us, her likeminded soul stitchers.

Sue Spargo

TABLE *of* CONTENTS

1	INTRODUCTION

QUILTING

5	WENSLEYDALE
15	POINT ADDIS
25	THIS WAY NOT THAT
36	HOMESTEAD
44	AUNT SUKEY'S
54	DIAMOND EXCHANGE
64	WINKI STARS
73	DAYLESFORD
92	LOVE LETTERS
97	TILLY'S BED
107	TOMAR
114	CLOPIN
121	CUSHION ASSEMBLY

BAKING

127   MUM'S SPONGE CAKE

131   LILLIAN'S DELICIOUS CHOCOLATE CAKE
134   *Whipped Chocolate Ganache*

140   OATMEAL RAISIN COOKIES

144   TASTY GINGER BISCUITS

150   SYRUP SOAKED ORANGE CAKE
151   *Glazed Orange Slices*

156   DELIGHTFUL POWDER PUFFS

161   MAISIE'S PASSION FRUIT SHORTCAKE

167   JILL'S TASTY CUPCAKES

172   JEN KINGWELL

173   TEMPLATES

183   ACKNOWLEDGEMENTS

Introduction

For me, food and quilts symbolise comfort… and I will be forever thankful to my mother for fostering the love of home and handmade. I was lucky to have the childhood I did, raised in a house of love. My mother was not a crafter but a wonderful baker and our home was filled with cakes and biscuits. I remember as a child being envious of others who had store-bought biscuits, not appreciating just how fortunate I was with the abundance of home baked goods I had. My dad loved dessert and hardly a night went by without one!

I grew up on a dairy farm. The kitchen was a large "eat-in" room with a wood fired oven. My mother loved the invention of the chest freezer and would bake and fill it to the brim. I would come home from school to the kitchen table laden with goodies. When unexpected visitors arrived my mother could provide the most amazing afternoon tea spread within minutes.

Over the years I have made copies of her recipes and love that each had a notation of who had provided the recipe to her. Also written are little notes e.g. "easy" or "keeps well".

The country way was all about community support and the delivery of food hampers was one way of showing this. From the birth of a new baby to the death of a loved one, a basket of goodies would be gifted with love. Quilts are often gifted in this same way. I look back now with such deep respect and the fondest memories of my mum.

Interior design has always been an interest of mine, and for reasons unknown to me quilts have often been overlooked by this industry. My vision for this book was to combine quilts with beautiful interiors and bring them into the homewares arena.

Wensleydale

I am known for my love of sampler style quilts but I equally love a single repeat block design and the symmetry and calm it brings. This block design plays on the rectangle and I find the effect very pleasing. A great block for a more masculine quilt design also.

Requirements

6 -7 mts (7- 8 yds) of a variety of small cuts of fabric - fat 8ths work well

3.8 mts (4 $\frac{1}{4}$ yds) backing fabric

55 cm ($\frac{5}{8}$ yd) binding fabric

190 cm x 205 cm (74" x 80") batting

Template plastic

Fine permanent marker and scissors for plastic

Fabric scissors

Fabric marking pencil e.g. Sewline

Sandpaper board

Simple seam wheel or ruler with $\frac{1}{4}$" seam markings

Cotton thread to blend

General sewing supplies e.g. pins, needles, etc.

Sewing machine and rotary cutting equipment (optional)

* An acrylic template set is available for this design. Please ask your local quilt store.

Cutting

For each block cut:

1 of Template A from fabric 1

2 of Template B from fabric 2

2 of Template C from fabric 2

2 of Template D from fabric 3

2 of Template D in reverse from fabric 3

2 of Template E from fabric 4

2 of Template F from fabric 4

2 of Template G from fabric 5

2 of Template G in reverse from fabric 5

WENSLEYDALE

#wensleydalequilt

Finished block measures: 11" x 7 ¼" (27.9 cm x 18.5 cm)
Finished quilt measures: 66" x 72.5" (167.6 cm x 184 cm)

The addition of checks, plaids, geometrics and florals make this quilt perfect for anyone!

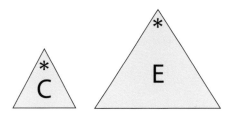

Note - When cutting Template C and E it will help if you mark the registration marks in your seam allowance. These triangles are not equilateral so this mark helps you get it in the correct position first time!

Assembly

Take Template A fabric and stitch Template B and C to the sides as follows:

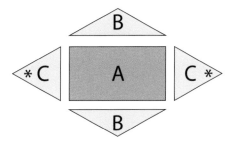

Note registration mark placement.

If you are hand piecing you can stitch this in one continuous seam.

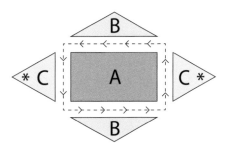

If machine piecing, stitch Template B to each side - press seam allowance toward B then stitch Template C to each end. Press seam allowance toward Template C.

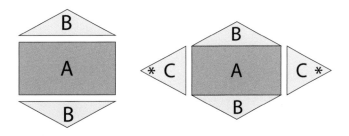

Next take Template D and D reversed and stitch to the A/B/C unit.

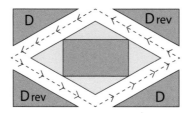

Hand piecing continuous seam. Machine piecing sequence.

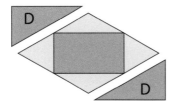 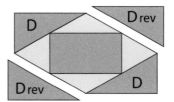

Press seam allowance to the outer edge of the block.

These sequences will apply to each round specific to hand or machine piecing.

Next take Template F and stitch to each side of the previously made unit.

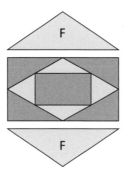

Then Template E to each end, noting registration marks.

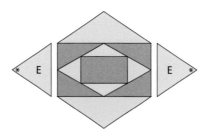

WENSLEYDALE

Lastly, add Template G and G reversed to the block - stitching in your preferred manner.

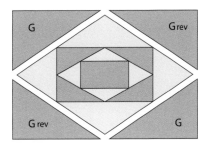

Press all seam allowances toward the outer edge of the block.
Your block is now complete.

Make as many blocks as you desire. I made 60 blocks and set them 6 blocks across x 10 blocks down giving a quilt which measures 66" x 72.5" (167.6 cm x 184 cm).

Lay out blocks to get an even and pleasing distribution of the print and colour.
Stitch blocks together to form rows, then stitch rows together.

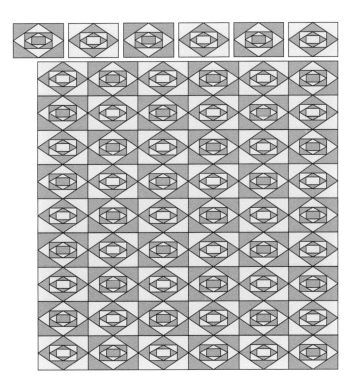

Quilt and bind as desired. Cuddle up and enjoy!

Point Addis

A one block wonder; I love this block and how trailing fabrics from one block to the next creates an interesting effect. Template cut but may be hand or machine pieced and does include inset seams.

Requirements

For each block you will need 25 cms ($1/4$ yd) of both feature and background fabric; there will be a little left over.

4 mts (4 $1/2$ yds) backing fabric

55 cm ($5/8$ yd) binding fabric

2 metre square (80") batting

Template plastic
Fine permanent marker and scissors for plastic
Scissors for fabric
Sandpaper board
Fabric marking pencil e.g. Sewline
Simple seam wheel or ruler with $1/4$" markings
Cotton thread to blend
General sewing supplies: pins, needles, etc.
Sewing machine (optional)
Rotary cutting equipment (optional)

* An acrylic template set is available for this design. Please ask your local quilt store.

Cutting

Before cutting fabric you will need to make the decision if you want one block to lead into the next as in the featured quilt.

For each block cut:

From focus fabric:

1 x Template A
2 x Template C
6 x Template D
4 x Template G

From background fabric:

8 x Template B
2 x Template E
2 x Template E reversed
4 x Template F
4 x Template F reversed
4 x Template H
4 x Template H reversed

POINT ADDIS

#pointaddisquilt

Finished block measures: 35.5 cm (14") square
Finished quilt measures: 178 cm (70") square

Assembly

Take Template A and stitch Template B to each side. If hand piecing, this can be done with one continuous seam.

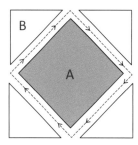 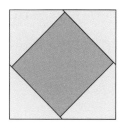

If machine piecing, stitch diagonally opposite corners. Press, then stitch the remaining sides.

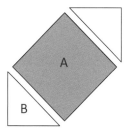 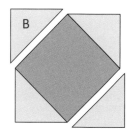 

Take Template C and stitch Template B to each side. Make 2 units. If hand piecing, this can be stitched as one continuous seam. If machine piecing, stitch one side. Press and then stitch the remaining side.

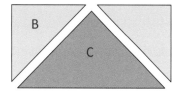 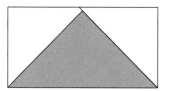

Take Template D and stitch a Template E to one side and Template E reversed to the opposite side, following methods above for hand piecing or machine piecing.
Make 2 units.

POINT ADDIS

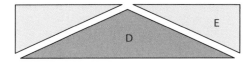 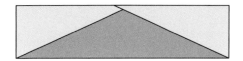

Take remaining D Templates and stitch Template F and F reversed to either side.

Make 4 units.

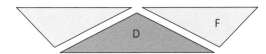 

Take Template G and stitch Template H and H reversed to either side.

Make 4 units.

Once all units are stitched you can start the block construction.

Take the A/B unit and stitch a C/B unit to 2 sides. Next, stitch a D/E unit to the opposite sides of previously made unit.

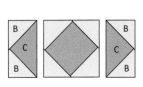 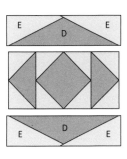 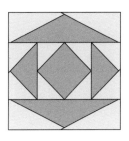

Take the D/F and G/H units and stitch together in pairs.

Make 4 units.

POINT ADDIS

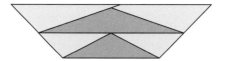

Stitch block together as follows. Note - Remember to leave ¼" seam allowance unstitched at points marked with • as this is an inset seam.

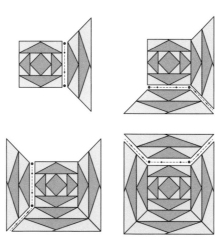

Make the desired number of blocks to achieve the size of quilt required.
This quilt is set 5 blocks across by 5 blocks down - a total of 25 blocks.

Set out in rows. Stitch blocks together into rows, then stitch rows together to complete the quilt top.

Quilt and bind as desired. Enjoy!

QUILT RECIPES | 19

This Way Not That

A simple machine pieced quilt to showcase large graphic prints, or make in solids for a sleek modern effect. This quilt is rotary cut and machine pieced, therefore $1/4$" seam allowance is included in all cutting instructions. Please read the pattern before beginning.

Requirements

3.3 mts (3 $5/8$ yds) total of feature fabrics - fat 8ths work well for variety

1.8 mts (2 yds) dark fabric for corner triangles

1.8 mts (2 yds) light fabric for corner triangles

3.6 mts (4 yds) backing fabric

180 cm (70") square batting

55 cm ($5/8$ yd) binding fabric

Rotary cutter, mat and ruler

Sewing machine with $1/4$" foot

Cotton thread to blend

General sewing supplies - pins, scissors, etc.

Cutting

From feature fabrics cut:

77 squares at 7 $1/2$"

8 rectangles at 7 $1/2$" x 4"

From dark corner fabric cut:

162 squares at 4"

From light corner fabric cut:

162 squares at 4"

#thiswaynotthatquilt

Finished block measures: 17.7 cm (7" square)
Finished quilt measures: 160 cm (63") square, or as desired.

Assembly

First you need to mark a diagonal line on the wrong side of all the 4" squares.
You can press or draw this - whichever method suits.

Take a square of feature fabric and place 2 light squares on diagonally opposite corners.
Place fabrics right sides together and stitch on the diagonal line.

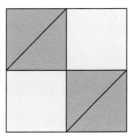

Trim the corner off leaving a ¼" seam allowance. Press triangle up to complete square.

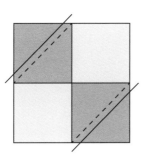 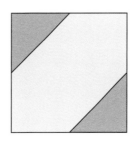

Next, take the dark squares cut at 4" and place right sides together on the diagonally opposite corners.

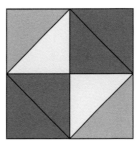

Stitch on the drawn lines and trim off corners leaving a ¼" seam allowance. Press.

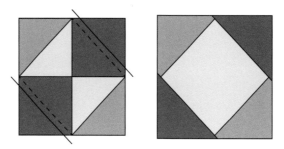

Make 77 blocks in this manner.

Take the rectangles cut at 7 ½" x 4" and place a light square to one side, stitch on the diagonal line. Trim leaving a ¼" seam allowance and press.

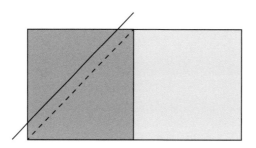

Next, place a dark square on the other side of the rectangle and stitch on the diagonal line. Trim and press as before.

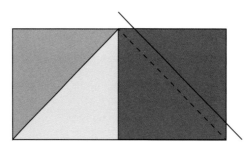

Make 4 units with the light square to the left and 4 units with the light square to the right.

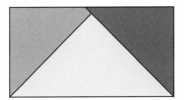 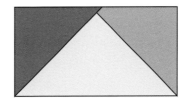

Lay squares out in rows to get an even mix of print and colour. You will have 5 rows containing 9 blocks, and 4 rows containing 8 blocks with a half block at each end.

Note the orientation of the corner triangles as you lay these out.

Once you are happy with the layout, stitch blocks together into rows, then stitch rows together to complete the quilt top.

Quilt and bind as desired. Enjoy!

HOMESTEAD

#homesteadquilt

Finished quilt measures: 167.5 cm x 195.5 cm (66" x 77")

Homestead

This quilt is a quick and easy machine sewn project. It gives graphic impact with large blocks of colour. Inspired by a floor rug design, I thought it was a perfect design for my new couch cuddle quilt. These instructions are written for rotary cutting and machine piecing. Therefore, all seam allowances are $1/4"$ and are included in the cutting instructions.

Requirements

40 cm (15") of 7 solid fabrics

2.7 mts (3 yds) of background fabric

2 mts ($2\,1/4$ yds) of charcoal fabric (includes binding)

3.8 mts ($4\,1/3$ yds) backing fabric

188 cm x 215 cm (74" x 85") batting

Rotary cutter, mat and ruler (with 45° angle markings)

Cotton thread to blend

Sewing machine with $1/4"$ foot

General sewing requirements e.g. pins, scissors, tape measure, etc.

Aurifil 12 wt thread for hand quilting (optional)

Cutting

From each of the coloured fabrics cut the following:

3 rectangles at $18\,1/2"$ x $3\,1/2"$

2 rectangles at $12\,1/2"$ x $3\,1/2"$

1 square at $3\,7/8"$

Cut once on the diagonal to yield 2 triangles

2 squares at $7\,1/4"$

Cut twice on the diagonal to yield 8 triangles

From background fabric cut the following:

Cut fabric length at 180 cm (70")

Then cut 16 strips at $1\,1/2"$ down the length of the fabric (along the selvedge)

Trim these to measure $1\,1/2"$ x $66\,1/2"$

Cut these first and pop aside

From remaining background fabric cut:

37 squares at $7\,1/4"$

2 squares at $3\,7/8"$

From charcoal fabric:

2 strips at $2\,1/2"$ x length of fabric - cut these first and pop aside

3 rectangles at $18\,1/2"$ x $3\,1/2"$

2 rectangles at $12\,1/2"$ x $3\,1/2"$

3 squares at $3\,7/8"$

13 squares at $7\,1/4"$

(The remaining charcoal fabric can be used for binding).

Assembly

The body of the quilt is made up of 2 rows only.

Make 8 x Row 1 and 7 x Row 2. I made an uneven number so the rows ended symmetrically with Row 1.

I just found this more pleasing to the eye. (Requirements allow for 8 rows of each).

Take the 18 $\frac{1}{2}$" x 3 $\frac{1}{2}$" rectangles and fold in half right sides together.

Lay your ruler with the 45° angle along the bottom edge.

Extend the ruler past the edge of the strip by $\frac{1}{4}$" - line up markings on the ruler.

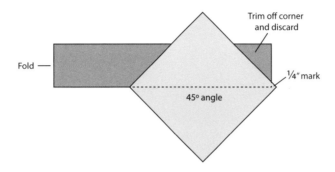

Trim corner. Make sure you do not cut the fold. Open strips and you should have a strip like this:

Note - All 18 $\frac{1}{2}$" rectangles are cut in this manner.

Next, take the 12 $\frac{1}{2}$" rectangles and trim one end in the manner described above. You will need to make a mirror image pair of each colour. This can be done by laying rectangles with right sides together and trimming one end only.

Row 1:

Layout fabric then stitch together into rows measuring 66 $\frac{1}{2}$" x 3 $\frac{1}{2}$".

Note - the triangles of both coloured and background fabric are cut from the 7 $\frac{1}{4}$" square.

The small end triangles are cut from the 3 $\frac{7}{8}$" square.

Row 2:

Press seams toward dark fabric.

Make one of Row 1 and one Row 2 from each coloured fabric.

Lay out rows alternating Row 1 and Row 2 with a strip of background fabric cut at $1\frac{1}{2}$" x $66\frac{1}{2}$" between each row.

Adjust colours until you are happy with the balance.

Row 1
Background
Row 2
Background
Row 1
Background
Row 2
Background
Row 1
Background
Row 2
Background
Row 1
Background
Row 2
Background
Row 1
Background
Row 2
Background
Row 1
Background
Row 2
Background
Row 1
Background
Row 2
Background
Row 1

Match the centre of the strip/row. Stitch rows together.

Stitch a background strip to the top and bottom of the quilt top.

Next take the background triangles (cut from $7\frac{1}{4}$" squares) and the charcoal triangles and make 2 rows as follows:

These rows will contain 11 charcoal triangles and 10 background triangles. Stitch a small background triangle to each end.

HOMESTEAD

Repeat to make 2 rows containing 11 background triangles and 10 charcoal triangles, adding small charcoal triangles each end.

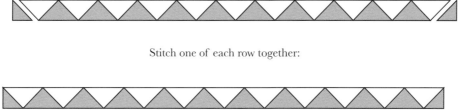

Stitch one of each row together:

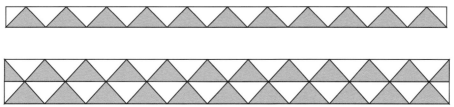

Make 2 units.
Stitch one to the top and one to the bottom of the quilt.
Take the long strips previously cut from charcoal fabric and trim to measure 2 ½" x 66 ½".
Stitch one to the top and one to the bottom.

Your quilt top is now complete! Baste, quilt and bind as desired. Cuddle up and enjoy!

This quilt is a great stash buster!

AUNT SUKEY'S

#auntsukeysquilt

Finished block measures: 30.5 cm (12") square
Finished quilt measures: 157 cm x 193 cm (62" x 76")

Aunt Sukey's

A classic block that I have loved for years. Can be made in a limited or scrappy palette. Blocks may be joined edge to edge or sashed as I have done.

The instructions for this pattern are written for rotary cutting and machine piecing, therefore all seam allowances are $1/4"$ and are included in the cutting instructions.

Requirements

1.8 mts (2 yds) fabric for sashing and borders
2.5 mts (2 7/8 yds) coloured fabric for blocks - fat 16ths work well for variety
2.3 mts (2 5/8 yds) background fabrics
3.6 mts (4 yds) backing fabric
180 cm x 210 cm (70" x 84") batting
55 cm (5/8 yd) binding fabric
Rotary cutter, mat and ruler
Sewing machine with 1/4" foot
General sewing supplies e.g. pins, scissors, etc.

Cutting

For each block cut:

From background fabric:
20 squares x 2 1/2" x 2 1/2"
4 rectangles x 2 1/2" x 4 1/2"

From coloured fabric:
16 squares at 2 1/2" x 2 1/2"
4 rectangles at 2 1/2" x 4 1/2"

Assembly for each block

Take a rectangle of coloured fabric and 2 squares of background fabric and create a Flying Geese rectangle, as follows. Make 4 units total.

Take the squares and draw a diagonal line on the wrong side.
Place one square, right sides together, on the rectangle.

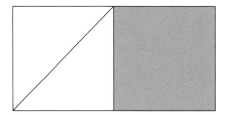

Stitch on the line and trim off corner, leaving a ¼" seam allowance.

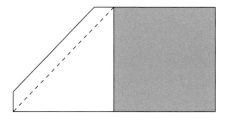

Flip and press seam allowance to the outer edge of block.

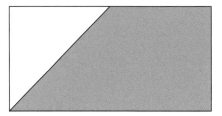

Repeat with the remaining square on the opposite side.

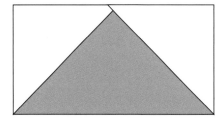

AUNT SUKEY'S

Repeat with the background rectangles and coloured squares.

Make 4 units total.

Layout the units for the block as follows - getting an even mix of colour and print.

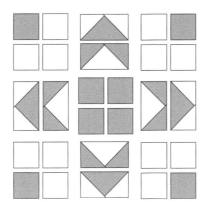

Stitch units together.

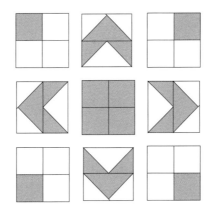

Stitch together in rows as you would a 9-patch.

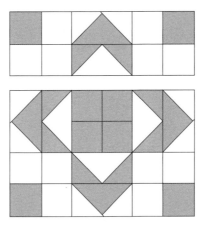

Make the desired number of blocks. This quilt features 20 blocks in total.

Sashing and borders

Cutting from the 1.8 mts down the length of your fabric (along the selvedge).
Cut 4 strips at 4 $\frac{1}{2}$" x the length.
Pop these aside for your borders.

From the remaining fabric cut strips 2 $\frac{1}{2}$" wide and sub cut these into 12 $\frac{1}{2}$" x 2 $\frac{1}{2}$" sashing strips. You need 31 in total.
From coloured fabrics. Cut 12 squares at 2 $\frac{1}{2}$" x 2 $\frac{1}{2}$" for posts.

Assembly of quilt top

Lay out your completed blocks making sure you get an even distribution of colour and print.
4 blocks across x 5 blocks down.
Stitch blocks together with a sashing strip between.

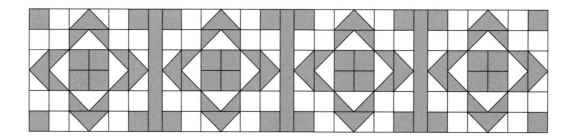

Make 5 rows containing 4 blocks and 3 sashing strips.
Next take 4 sashing strips and stitch with a coloured post between (3 in total).

Make 4 sashing rows in total. Stitch rows of blocks and sashing/post rows together.

AUNT SUKEY'S

Take 2 of the borders you have previously cut at 4 ½" wide and cut these to measure 4 ½" x 68 ½". Stitch these to each side of the quilt top.

Trim the remaining 2 border strips to measure 4 ½" x 62 ½" and stitch to the top and bottom of the quilt top. Quilt and bind as desired.

We all have a stash of fabric we love!
Use these to cut these large diamonds and enjoy them.

DIAMOND EXCHANGE

#diamondexchangequilt

Finished diamond measures: 33 cm x 17.75 cm (13" x 7") at the widest points
Finished quilt measures: 165 cm x 195 cm (65" x 77")

Diamond Exchange

This quilt is great for showcasing your favourite fabrics. Large templates make for easy piecing and it may be stitched by hand or machine.

Requirements

For each diamond you need 1 fat 8th of fabric (there will be a little left over)

1.1 mts (1 ¼ yds) of fabric for setting triangles/edges

3.8 mts (4 ⅓ yds) backing fabric

55 cm (⅝ yd) binding fabric

185 cm x 215 cm (73" x 85") batting

Template plastic

Fine permanent marker and scissors for plastic

Scissors for fabric

Fabric marking pencil e.g. Sewline

Simple seam wheel or ruler with ¼" markings

Sandpaper board

Cotton thread to blend

General sewing supplies e.g. pins, needles, etc.

Aurifil 12 wt thread for hand quilting (optional)

Sewing machine (optional)

* An acrylic template set is available for this design. Please ask your local quilt store.

Cutting

You may wish to alternate dark and light diamonds as I have.

For each diamond cut:

2 x Template A from a feature fabric

1 x Template B from a contrast fabric

To finish quilt cut:

24 x Template C

8 x Template D

Note - C and D are cut from fabric for setting triangles

Assembly

Take the 2 pieces of fabric cut from Template A and clip ⅛" into the seam allowance at the 'V'. This allows the seam to open slightly and sit flat at the pivot point.

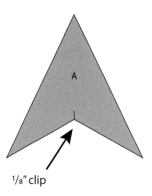

Stitch Template B fabric between the A fabrics, pivoting at the clipped mark.

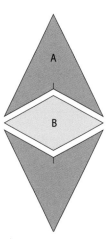

If machine stitching, you may find it easier to stitch from the centre of A to the edge. Then repeat on the opposite side, lowering your needle at the very first stitch you stitched previously, and making sure you back stitch.

Make as many diamond blocks as you need for your desired quilt size. This quilt has 95 blocks set 11 blocks across x 5 blocks down (shorter alternate rows contain 4 blocks down).

The rows are stitched together on the diagonal. You will find by laying out your blocks on a design wall you can get an even distribution of colour and print before you start stitching.

DIAMOND EXCHANGE

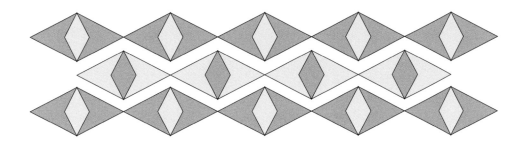

You may lay your diamonds horizontally (as photographed on page 53) or vertically (as per diagram below) depending on your preference/or make the quilt squarish, it doesn't matter.

I also find it less confusing if I lay my setting edge triangles out at this time, then I know I am stitching the correct pieces together.

You will make 7 diagonal rows containing 9 diamonds with Template C at each end (R1). Note registration mark on Template C *.

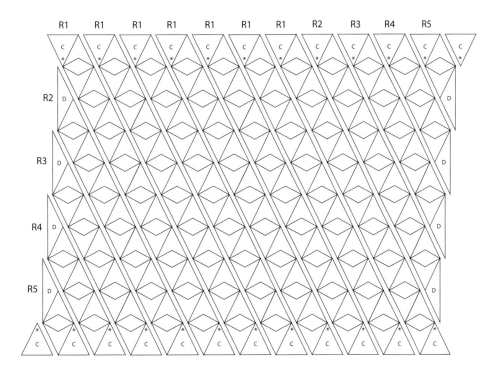

2 rows that commence with a Template D, contain 7 diamonds and finish with a Template C (R2).
2 rows that contain 5 diamonds and commence with a Template D and finish with a Template C (R3).
2 rows that contain 3 diamonds commencing and finishing as above (R4).
2 rows have 1 diamond and commence and finish as above (R5).

QUILT RECIPES / 56

DIAMOND EXCHANGE

Once all rows are stitched lay them out then stitch the long diagonal seams. Stitch the remaining Template C to the diagonally opposite corners to complete the quilt top. Trim all four corners, aligning your ruler with the edge of the quilt, remembering to leave the ¼" seam allowance intact as you trim.

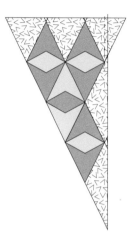

Baste and quilt as desired. If you wish to hand quilt, the template I used is included.

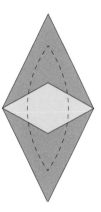

WINKI STARS

#winkistarsquilt

Finished block measures: 36.8 cm (14 ½") square
Finished quilt measures: 147 cm x 184 cm (58" x 72.5")

Winki Stars

This is a traditional star block that I chose to make with my "Winki Pop" fabric range. Fabric is cut using templates and I have written the instructions for hand piecing; however, it can also be machine pieced but does require inset seams.

Requirements

4 mts (4 １/２ yds) total of a variety of coloured fabric
3 mts (3 １/３ yds) background fabric
1.3 mts (1 １/２ yds) contrast fabric for star point
3.4 mts (3 ３/４ yds) backing fabric
55 cm (⅝ yd) binding fabric
170 cm x 205 cm (67" x 80") batting
Cotton thread to blend
Template plastic and permanent marking pen
Scissors for plastic
General sewing supplies e.g. pins, scissors, needles, etc.
Sandpaper board

* An acrylic template set is available for this design. Please ask your local quilt store.

Cutting

For each block:

From a variety of coloured fabric cut:
8 x Template A
12 x Template D

From background fabric cut:
8 x Template B
4 x Template C
4 x Template D

From star point fabric cut:
8 x Template B

Assembly

Make the 8-pointed star for the centre of the block as follows:

Take the 8 x Template A fabrics and stitch together in pairs.

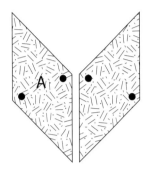

Make 4 units.

You need to leave the seam allowance unstitched at the junction marked with • as this becomes an inset seam.

Next, stitch the pairs together to create 2 half-star units.

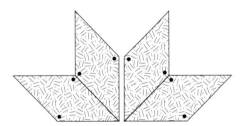

Then, stitch these units together across the centre seam.

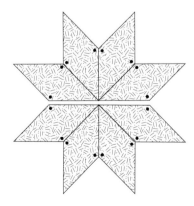

Take the Template B fabric cut from both the contrast star fabric and the background fabric and stitch these together down the long side.

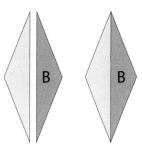

Make 8 units.

Then, stitch together in pairs, making sure to leave your seam allowance unstitched as this becomes an inset seam.

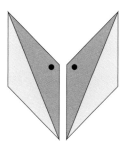

Make 4 units.

Take Template C cut from the background fabric and stitch Template D cut from the coloured fabric to two sides as follows:

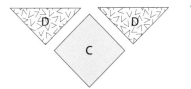 

Make 4 units.

Take one Template D cut from the background fabric and one cut from the coloured fabric and stitch together.

Make 4 units.

WINKI STARS

Take the 8-pointed star and stitch the 4 **BB** units into the corners as follows:

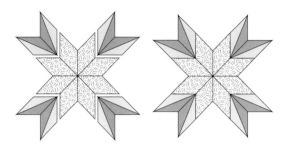

Next, take the remaining units and stitch together. This can be done as one continuous seam, if hand piecing.

Your block is now complete!

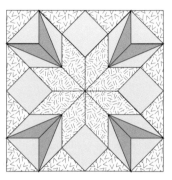

Make 20 blocks total and set your blocks 4 across and 5 down.

Quilt and bind as desired. Enjoy!

QUILT RECIPES / 69

Daylesford

This quilt is a choose-your-own-adventure of all my loves rolled into one:
medallion style, sampler - variety of blocks, log cabin, seminole and scrappy.

I was going to call it "The Scrappy Log Cabin Medallion Seminole Sampler" but that was a bit long!
I am giving the measurements for each panel and for making several different blocks.
You can choose where you place the blocks and how many to include, if any. This will make your quilt uniquely yours.

It is a great stash buster, and the fabric requirements will depend on how many different fabrics you choose to include
and how many pieced blocks you make.

The instructions for this quilt are written for rotary cutting and machine piecing. Therefore all seam allowances
are $1/4$" and are included in the cutting instructions.

Requirements

7 - 8 mts (7 $2/3$ - 8 $3/4$ yds) of fabric in total
25 cm ($1/4$ yd) and 50 cm ($1/2$ yd) cuts work well
4 mts (4 $1/2$ yds) backing fabric
55 cm ($5/8$ yd) binding fabric
Rotary cutter, ruler and mat
Sewing machine with $1/4$" foot
Cotton thread to blend
General sewing supplies e.g. pins, scissors, tape measure, etc.

DAYLESFORD

#daylesfordquilt

Finished quilt measures: 173 cm x 178 cm (68" x 70")

Half Square Triangle (HST)

2" finished (2 1/2" including seam allowance)

Cutting

1 square of light fabric at 2 7/8"

1 square of contrast or dark fabric at 2 7/8"

Assembly

Take 1 square of coloured and 1 square of light fabric cut at 2 7/8". Place right sides together. Draw a diagonal line on the wrong side of the lighter square. Stitch with a 1/4" seam allowance on each side of the drawn line.

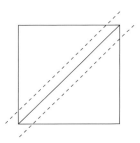

Cut on the diagonal line. Press seam allowance open as this will help reduce bulky seams.
This will make 2 half square triangle units.

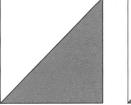 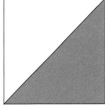

This quilt has 10 HST units in panel 1 and 4.

Churndash

3" finished (3 ½" including seam allowance)

Cutting

For each block cut:

2 squares of background fabric at 1 ⅞"
2 squares of feature fabric at 1 ⅞"
4 rectangles of background fabric at 1 ½" x 1"
4 rectangles of feature fabric at 1 ½" x 1"
1 centre square at 1 ½"

Assembly

Take the 2 squares of background fabric cut at 1 ⅞" and draw a diagonal line on the wrong side. Place a feature fabric square and background square right sides together. Stitch with a ¼" seam allowance on each side of the drawn line. Cut on the line and press seam toward darker fabric.

You should now have 4 half square triangle units.

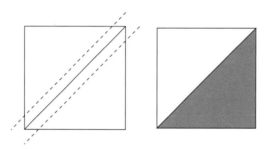

Take a rectangle of each fabric and stitch with right sides together to create a square.
Make 4 units. Press seam allowance to dark fabric.

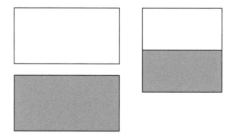

Assemble block in 3 rows as follows.

DAYLESFORD

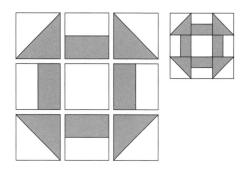

This quilt has 10 Churndash blocks used in panel 30.

Square in a Square

3" finished (3 $\frac{1}{2}$" including seam allowance)

Cutting

For each block:

From fabric A cut one square at 3 $\frac{1}{2}$"

From fabric B cut 4 squares at 2"

Assembly

Take a square of fabric which will be the centre of your block. This square will be the size of your finished block plus seam allowance e.g. 3" finished cut 3 $\frac{1}{2}$" square.

Take 4 small squares of a contrast fabric and mark a diagonal line on the wrong side of each.

Place 2 squares on diagonally opposite corners of centre square and stitch on marked line. Cut off corners leaving $\frac{1}{4}$" seam allowance.

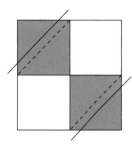

Press, then repeat with remaining corners.

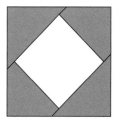

This quilt has 4 Square in a Square units in panel 7.

QUILT RECIPES | 79

Flying Geese

4" x 2" finished (4 ½" x 2 ½" including seam allowance)

Cutting

Cut 2 rectangles at 2 ½" x 4 ½"

Cut 4 squares at 2 ½"

Assembly

Draw a diagonal line on the wrong side of the squares.

Place one square, right sides together, on the rectangle, noting the direction of the diagonal line.

Stitch on the line and trim off corner, leaving ¼" seam allowance.

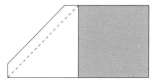

Flip and press seam allowance to the outer edge of block.

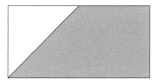

Repeat with the remaining square on the opposite side.

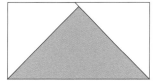

This quilt has 8 Flying Geese units used in panel 14.

Window Panel

4" finished (4 $\frac{1}{2}$" including seam allowance)

Cutting

Use two contrasting fabrics.

From fabric 1 cut:

2 strips at 2" x width of fabric

2 strips at 1 $\frac{1}{2}$" x width of fabric

From fabric 2 cut:

1 strip at 1 $\frac{1}{2}$" x width of fabric

Assembly

Take the strip of fabric 2 and stitch the strips of fabric 1 cut at 2" to the either side.

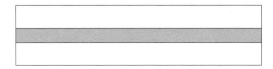

Press seams toward fabric 1.

Sub cut this strip into segments measuring 2".

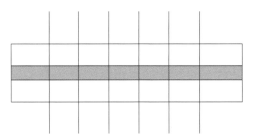

Take the strips of fabric 1 cut at 1 $\frac{1}{2}$" and cut into segments measuring 1 $\frac{1}{2}$" x 4 $\frac{1}{2}$".

Stitch units together as follows:

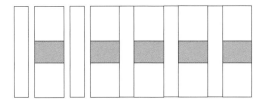

Make to the desired length.

This quilt has 11 of the pieced "windows" and 12 vertical strips used in panel 16.

Pinwheels

4" finished (4 ½" including seam allowance)

Follow the instructions for the 2" HST units.

You will need to make 36 HST units.

Make up as follows:

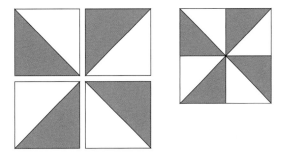

This quilt has 9 pinwheels used in panel 21.

Bow Border

4" finished (4 ½" including seam allowance)

Cutting

Cut rectangles at 4 ½" x 2 ½"

Cut contrasting squares at 2 ½"

Assembly

Draw a diagonal line on the wrong side of the squares.

Position a square on a rectangle with right sides together and stitch on the drawn line as follows:

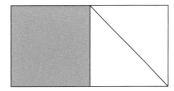

Trim excess from corner leaving a ¼" seam allowance. Flip and press.

DAYLESFORD

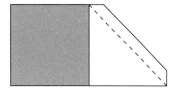 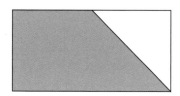

Make 2 of the above units for each 4" finished square.

Stitch together as follows:

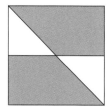

This quilt has 9 Bow blocks used in panel 37.

Strip Border

4" finished width (4 $\frac{1}{2}$" including seam allowance)

From a variety of fabric cut strips at 1 $\frac{1}{2}$" x 4 $\frac{1}{2}$" and stitch down the long sides.

Make to desired length.

This quilt has 39 strips used in panel 32.

9 Patch

5" finished width (5 $\frac{1}{2}$" including seam allowance)

Cutting

From background fabric cut 5 strips at 1 $\frac{1}{2}$" x WOF

From fabric 1 cut 3 strips at 1 $\frac{1}{2}$" x WOF

From contrast fabric cut 1 strip at 1 $\frac{1}{2}$" x WOF

Assembly

Take 2 strips of background fabric and stitch to either side of a fabric 1 strip.

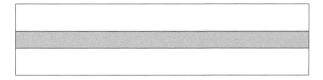

Subcut this into units measuring 1 $\frac{1}{2}$".

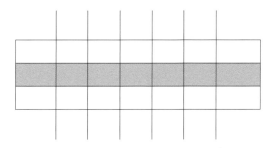

Take 2 strips of fabric 1 and stitch to either side of the contrast fabric strip.

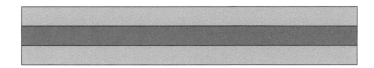

Subcut this into units measuring 1 $\frac{1}{2}$".

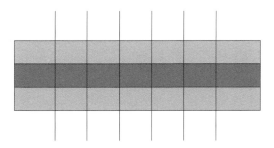

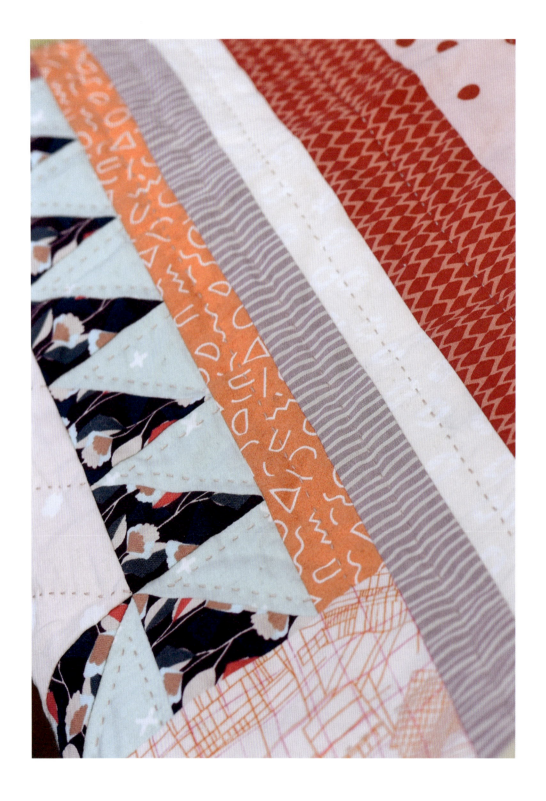

Take 1 background strip and cut into segments measuring 1 ½" x 3 ½".
Stitch the pieced unit as follows to create a 9 patch block.

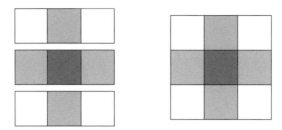

Stitch these units together with a strip of background fabric between them.

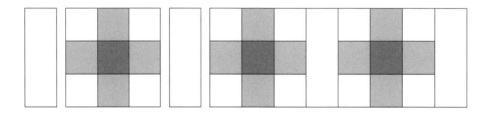

This quilt has 9 x 9 patch blocks with 10 strips used in panel 23.

Once you have made your strip of 9 patch blocks to the desired length, stitch the remaining strips of background fabric to each side. These will be cut to the length of your strip of 9 patch blocks.

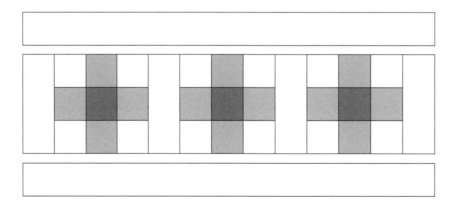

Quilt Assembly

Starting with a centre square cut at 10 ½", I worked in a counterclockwise direction. The measurements given in each border are the finished measurement, followed by the cut measurement in brackets i.e. finished (unfinished).

DAYLESFORD

If you are piecing a segment within the border you will need to calculate how much you add to this strip to get the finished measurement.

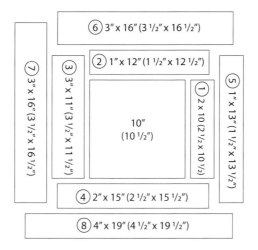

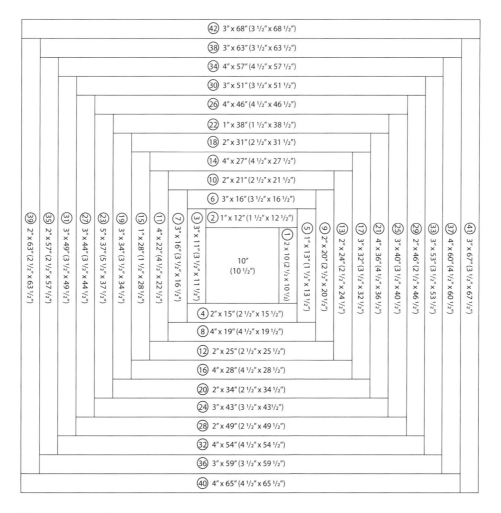

Diagram not to scale.

LOVE LETTERS

A great stash buster as small cuts of fabric are used.

#loveletterscushion

Finished block measures: 12.7 cm x 15.2 cm (5" x 6")

Finished cushion measures: 61 cm x 63.5 cm (24" x 25")

Love Letters

This versatile little pattern can be made to any size you desire. Imagine a cot quilt or a larger quilt made in masculine colours. The instructions for this pattern are written for rotary cutting and machine piecing. Therefore, all seam allowances are $1/4$" and are included in the cutting instructions.

Requirements

15 cm (6") fabric for centre rectangle in total or small cuts for variety

60 cm ($2/3$ yd) of coloured fabrics in total

70 cm ($3/4$ yd) backing fabric

70 cm (28") square batting (if quilting)

25 cm (10") binding fabric (optional)

Rotary cutter, mat and ruler

Sewing machine with $1/4$" foot

Cotton thread to blend

General sewing supplies e.g. pins, tape measure, scissors, etc.

50 cm (20") zip if making a cushion

Aurifil 12 wt thread for hand quilting (optional)

Cutting

For each block cut:

1 x rectangle 3 $1/2$" x 2 $1/2$" for centre

From each of four coloured fabrics cut:

1 x square at 2"

1 x rectangle at 2" x 3"

Assembly

Lay out the fabric.

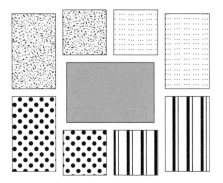

Stitch the 2" squares together.

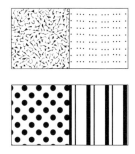

Stitch the rectangles together.

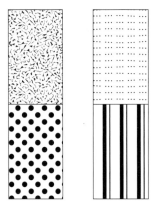

Then stitch the units together as follows.

LOVE LETTERS

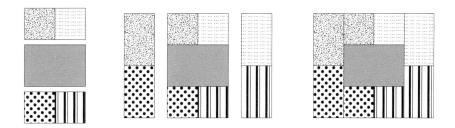

Make the desired numbers of blocks. For the cushion, you will require 20 blocks.

Set 4 blocks across by 5 rows down.

Stitch together in rows.

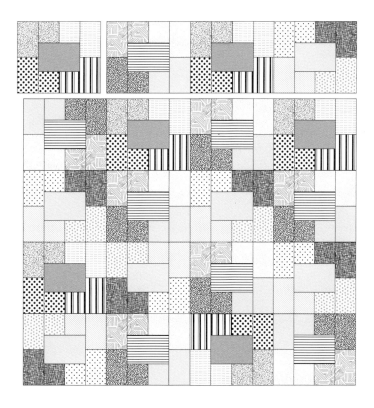

Baste and quilt as desired.

Bind or finish as a cushion - see instructions on page 121.

QUILT RECIPES / 94

The star of the show: Our family dog Matilda - aka Tilly, Tilda, Schnoogy Bear, the list goes on!

Tilly's Bed

The art of chenille is age old. Dare I say I had a gorgeous chenille bedspread in the 60's. I wish I could remember who taught me this technique. I'm sorry I can't. I know it was at Quilt Market in Houston in the early 2000's, but who was demonstrating, I don't know.

Requirements

These will depend on how many colours you wish to chenille and the size of the dog bed or cushion. Fat quarters work well.

Background fabric for cushion top (size dependant)

Fabric for base and walled gusset (size dependant)

Rotary cutter, ruler and mat

Sewing machine with zipper foot

Zip - size appropriate for the base of the cushion

Fusible batting (optional)

Cotton threads to match

General sewing requirements e.g. pins, tape measure, scissors, etc.

Nylon brush with stiff bristles

TILLY'S BED

#tillysdogbed

Finished cushion measures: As desired

Instructions to make "Chenille"

Take a fat quarter and fold right-sides out on the diagonal to create a triangle. Mark lines a $\frac{1}{2}$" apart using either a marker and ruler or use the stitch guide on your sewing machine. Stitch with a matching thread colour on these diagonal lines.

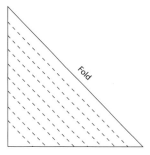

Cut $\frac{1}{2}$" wide strips by cutting between the stitching lines.

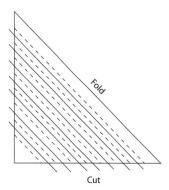

Make these $\frac{1}{2}$" bias strips from as many coloured fabrics as you wish to use. I find solids work the best for this.

Take your background piece of fabric. Oversize the measurement by 1" wider as the stitching does "shrink" the background a little. You can trim this back to size when you have finished stitching your chenille design.

Mark your design on the background fabric. You can truly make any design you like, as the strips are cut on the bias they curve beautifully.
You might like to cut out flower petals and then stitch the chenille around the edges.

If you are appliquéing a piece of fabric to your background, I suggest that you stitch it in place with a zig-zag stitch as this will prevent the edges of your appliqué from fraying with the brushing process. These edges will then be covered with the chenille and the zig zag will be hidden.

You can start anywhere in the design; it doesn't matter if you stitch from the centre out or the outside in.

Jen's Tip

Make sure you back stitch and secure each end of every strip of chenille very well.

Stitch the first strip of chenille onto the background fabric along the previously stitched line.

Fold back so as not to stitch down the edge and stitch the second strip. Continue around the diamond.

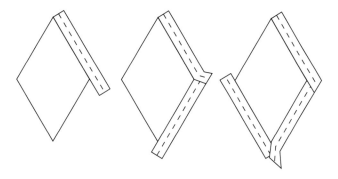

When adding the second and following rounds, fold the previously stitched strips out of the way and line the cut edge of the next piece beside the stitched edge. Continue around the shape until you have enough rows of chenille to complete your design.

Examples

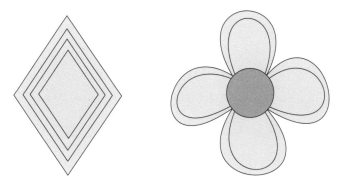

Once all the design is stitched in place take a stiff brush and "rough" up the edges of the chenille strips. You can also place the whole piece in the washing machine and dryer if preferred, but make sure all the outside edges have been overlocked.

TILLY'S BED

Make up your piece of chenille as desired.

You can use this technique on cushions, quilts etc. How cute would it look around the edge of a quilt after you have stitched the binding - just add one row of chenille stitched on top!

Tilly's Dog Bed

Take your chenille panel and iron on batting to the wrong side.
Place a piece of fabric behind the batting and quilt as desired.

Trim piece to size plus 1". It's best to stitch this project with a $\frac{1}{2}$" seam allowance.
Make up a backing panel following the instructions on page 121 with zip inserted.
Trim to the exact size of your cushion top or chenille panel.

Add the 4 side measurements together and add 6" to this length. Cut the gusset strip to this length and to the height that you want your dog bed to sit e.g. 4", add 1" seam allowance = 5"
You might like to quilt this piece with batting and backing as this gives a good sturdy side wall to your cushion.

Stitch the gusset strip onto your cushion top. Starting near the centre of one side stitch with right sides together.
Leave 3" of the gusset strip free at the beginning.

Remember, you are stitching with a $\frac{1}{2}$" seam allowance.

When you reach the corner, stop stitching $\frac{1}{2}$" before the end.
Leave the needle down in the fabric. Snip a $\frac{1}{4}$" into the gusset strip right at this junction.
Pivot around corner and align the next edges to be stitched.

Pull the bulk out of the way at the corner and stitch along the next side.

Continue around until you reach where you started leaving a 6" gap. Join the ends of the gusset strip together, making sure the gusset fits perfectly and lays smoothly along the cushion top. Trim excess then stitch the remaining length of seam.

Carefully mark the outer edge of the gusset strip at each corner making sure it is exactly opposite the previously stitched one.
This is important to get everything lined up and to stop the cushion top and bottom from "twisting".

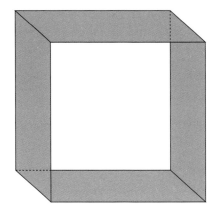

Pin the cushion base into this frame matching the pins to each corner and stitch in the same manner as you did when stitching the top in place.

Jen's Tip

Leave the zip undone 2" - 3" so you can turn your cushion right side out.

You may also like to overlock these seam edges as this doggie bed will be washed a lot - our Tilly is a grub!

Tomar

I love this simple, graphic design. So versatile. Make it as a cushion, table runner, placemats or stitch long rows together to create a quilt. Can be hand or machine pieced.

Requirements

25 cm (¼ yd) dark/contrast fabric
40 cm (½ yd) background fabric
50 cm (⅝ yd) backing fabric for cushion
Zipper to fit i.e. 40 cm (15")
Cotton thread to blend
Scrap of batting if you wish to quilt
Aurifil 12 wt thread for quilting (optional)
General sewing supplies e.g. pins, needles, etc.
Rotary cutter, mat and ruler
Template plastic
Fine permanent marker and scissors for plastic
Fabric marking pencil e.g. Sewline
Sewing machine (optional)

* An acrylic template set is available for this design. Please ask your local quilt store.

Cutting

From background fabric cut:
12 of Template A
1 rectangle at 24 ½" x 8"

From contrast fabric cut:
10 of Template A
2 of Template B and 2 Template B in reverse
2 strips at 1 ¼" x 24 ½"

#tomarcushion

Finished cushion measures: 43 cm x 61 cm (17" x 24")

Assembly

Take the contrast and background triangles cut from Template A and stitch with right sides together.

If machine stitching, press seam allowance to dark fabric then stitch the next triangle in place.
Repeat until you have stitched 6 background and 5 contrast triangles together.
If hand stitching, you can stitch this in one continuous seam.

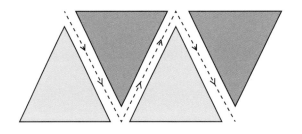

Make 2 strips containing 6 background and 5 contrast triangles.
Stitch a contrast Template B and B reverse to each end of both strips.

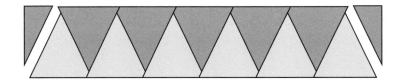

Lay your units out as follows.

TOMAR

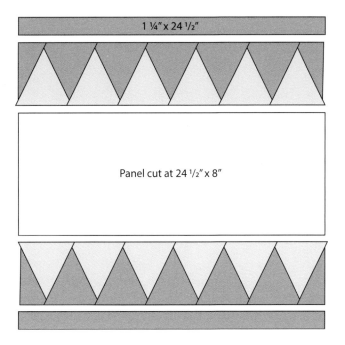

Take the 2 pieced strips and stitch to the top and bottom of the large panel, then stitch strips cut at 1 $^1/_4$".
Press and make up into a cushion following instructions on page 121, or quilt and bind as placemats.

Relax and enjoy!

#clopincushion

Finished cushion measures: 43 cm x 61 cm (17" x 24")

Clopin

When I finished this little piece and was searching for a name, I kept thinking of Clopin Trouillefou, a character in Disney's "Hunchback of Notre Dame" and the song "Topsy Turvy" was playing in my mind! This project can be hand or machine pieced.

Requirements

30 cm (1/3 yd) coloured fabrics - small cuts to give variety

50 cm (1/2 yd) background fabric

15 cm (6") charcoal fabric

50 cm (1/2 yd) backing fabric

50 cm (18") zip for cushion back (optional)

Template plastic

Permanent marker and scissors for plastic

Fabric scissors

Fabric marking pencil e.g. Sewline

General sewing supplies e.g. pins, needles, etc.

Cotton thread to blend

Scrap of batting if you wish to quilt

Sandpaper board

Simple seam wheel or ruler with 1/4" markings

Sewing machine (optional)

Aurifil 12 wt thread for hand quilting (optional)

* An acrylic template set is available for this design.
Please ask your local quilt store.

Cutting

From background fabric cut:

22 of Template A

2 of Template B

2 of Template B in reverse

32 of Template C

2 strips 24 1/2" x 1 1/2"

From a variety of coloured fabric cut:

24 of Template B

24 of Template B in reverse

From Charcoal fabric cut:

18 of Template D

Assembly

Take the Template B's cut from coloured fabrics and stitch a B and B reversed together as follows.

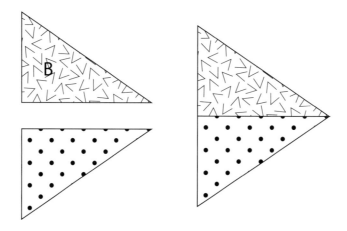

Make 24 units.

Take Template A cut from background fabric and stitch to a B unit.

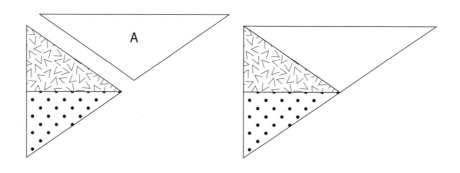

Make 22 units.

Stitch 2 of these units together as follows.

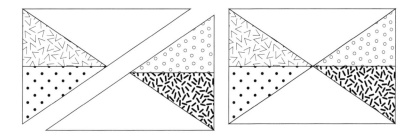

This will give 11 elongated hourglass units.
Next, take the remaining coloured B units and stitch a B and B reversed cut
from background fabric as follows.

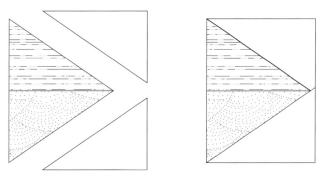

Make 2 units.
Take the charcoal diamonds cut from Template D and the Template C cut from background
fabric and stitch into long "sashing rows" as follows.

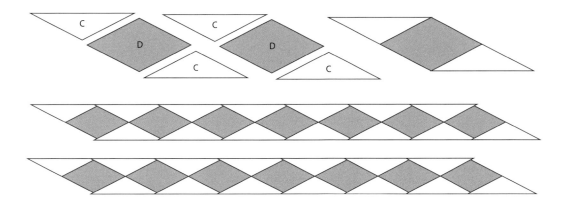

Stitch 2 rows with 7 diamonds.

Take the remaining Template D and stitch to the remaining Template C as follows.

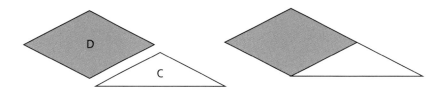

Make 4 units.

Stitch these to each end of the previously made sashing rows.

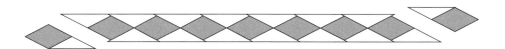

Trim off excess from Template D remembering to leave ¼" seam allowance each end of both rows.

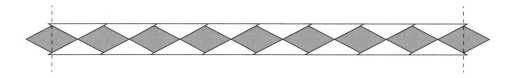

Lay out all previously made units.

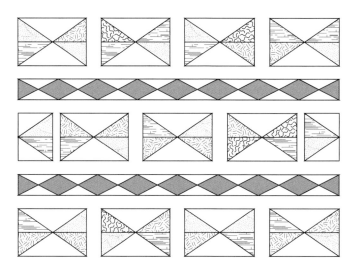

Stitch together in rows.

Take the 2 strips of background fabric cut at 24 ½" x 1 ½" and stitch

to the top and bottom of pieced unit.

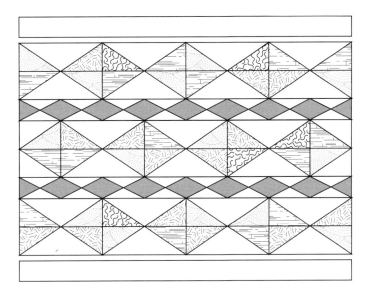

Baste and quilt if desired.

Make up the cushion following the instructions on page 121.

Relax and enjoy!

Cushion Assembly

This is a very simple and effective way to back your cushion.
Measure your front panel and cut your chosen backing fabric to match the height but add 2 - 3 inches to the length measurement.
Cut this panel into 2 pieces. I cut mine off centre as I like the effect.

Cut a strip 2" x cushion height measurement. This can be from the same fabric or contrasting fabric if desired.
Your zip should be around this measurement also or just slightly smaller.
Fold the 2" strip in half wrong sides together and press.
Take the larger rectangle, the folded strip and the zip. Lay out as follows:

CUSHION ASSEMBLY

Place the large rectangle right side facing you.
Lay the folded strip with cut edges along edge of rectangle then lay zip wrong side facing up with tab at bottom.
Aligning edges, with zipper foot attached to your machine, stitch close to the teeth on your zip.
Flip zip and folded strip over. Press.
The seam allowance will face the large rectangle. The zip should now sit under the folded strip.

Take the smaller rectangle and with right side facing the right side of zip, stitch close to the teeth.
Make sure you fold your strip out of the way. Press seam toward rectangle.
Your zip should be laying flat (hidden) beneath the folded strip.
Place cushion back right side facing up and lay the cushion front on top right sides
together - remember to open your zip 3 - 4" so you can turn your cushion right side out when stitched.

Using a $1/4$" seam allowance, stitch around the 4 sides. Trim excess from backing if necessary.
Turn right sides out. Press well and top stitch very close to the edge, if desired.
Another trick is to bind the edge of the cushion as you would bind a quilt.
This gives the effect of piping but is much easier to do.
I suggest you cut your binding strip just a little narrower e.g. 1 $1/2$" - 2" depending on the size of your cushion.
Smaller cushions need narrower binding for balance.

Your cushion is now complete!

Baking Recipes

Some very simple, yet delicious recipes to enjoy in between stitching, basting or quilting.

Mum's Sponge Cake

Prep Time: 10 minutes | Baking Time: 20 - 25 minutes

Ingredients

4 eggs

¾ cup castor sugar

¾ cup corn flour

1 tablespoon of custard powder

1 teaspoon cream of tartar

½ teaspoon of bicarb soda

1 dessert spoon plain flour

Method

Preheat oven to 180°C/350°F (fan forced).
Take 2 x 20 cm/8" round sponge tins, grease well,
line with baking paper and dust with a little extra flour.
Separate your egg yolks from the whites.
Sift dry ingredients and set aside.

Beat egg whites until soft peaks form, and add sugar gradually. Beat in egg yolks gently, until just combined.
Add dry ingredients and fold in gently with a spoon or spatula.

Divide mixture evenly between the two tins.
Place on the middle rack in your preheated oven.
Do not open the oven door while cooking!
Bake for 20 - 25 minutes.

Cool for a few minutes in the tins, then tip your sponges onto a wire cooling rack.

Ice with passion fruit icing (page 161) and fill with whipped cream.

This recipe was a constant growing up. Mum would make and freeze them unfilled or iced. They would appear effortlessly when unexpected visitors dropped in.

SPONGE CAKE

Jen's Tip

You will know they are cooked when the sponge pulls away from the edge of the tin. Do not test with a skewer or fork as this may deflate your sponge. To make a chocolate sponge, omit the plain flour and add a tablespoon of cocoa powder and sift with the dry ingredients.

Lillian's Delicious Chocolate Cake

Prep Time: 15 minutes | Baking Time: 60 minutes

Ingredients

¾ cup cocoa powder

220 g/7 oz butter (melted)

1 cup water

2 eggs

2 cups castor sugar

2 cups plain flour

1 teaspoon baking powder

1 teaspoon bicarb soda

180 g/6 oz sour cream

1 ½ teaspoons vanilla essence

Method

Preheat oven to 175°C/345°F (fan forced). Grease a 20 cm/8" cake tin and line the base with baking paper.

Sift all the dry ingredients together, then mix in all other ingredients.

Beat on high for 3 minutes or until combined. Pour mixture into cake tin and bake for 1 hour. Let it cool slightly before removing from tin and transfer to a wire rack.

Ice with whipped chocolate ganache (recipe on page 134) when completely cool and decorate as desired.

CHOCOLATE CAKE

CHOCOLATE CAKE

Whipped Chocolate Ganache

Ingredients

180 g/6 oz 70% cocoa chocolate

1 cup cream

Chop the chocolate really finely (this helps it melt to create a smoother ganache) and place in a heatproof bowl.

Heat cream in a saucepan over low heat but do not let it boil. Remove from the heat just as small bubbles form around the edge of the saucepan. Pour the cream over your chocolate and leave it to sit for 2 - 3 minutes to soften the chocolate. Then stir slowly with a metal spoon until combined.

Let your mixture cool completely on the bench. Once cooled, you can whip it with an electric or hand beater. I whisk the mixture until light in colour and 'fluffy' approximately 3 - 4 minutes. Spread generously over your cake and enjoy!

Jen's Tip

Whip the ganache before refrigerating as I find it can split a little if whipped when too cold.

CHOCOLATE CAKE

Many things my mum baked were delicious, but simply made.
This "all in together" chocolate cake is no exception. You may ice it with
whatever icing you like but my family like it with chocolate ganache.

Oatmeal Raisin Cookies

Prep Time: 15 minutes | Baking Time: 10 - 15 minutes | Makes: 24 large or 48 small

Ingredients

2 ½ cups rolled oats

2 cups plain flour

1 teaspoon baking powder

1 teaspoon bicarb soda

250 g/8.8 oz butter (softened)

2 eggs

1 teaspoon vanilla essence

1 cup sugar

1 cup brown sugar

1 - 2 cups of raisins (to taste) - can be swapped out for white or chocolate chips.

120 g/4.2 oz macadamia nuts (roughly chopped) - may be omitted if desired.

Method

Preheat your oven to 175°C/345° F (fan forced) and line your baking trays with baking paper or a biscuit sheet.

Cream butter, sugar and brown sugar on high in a large mixing bowl for approximately 10 minutes or until light and fluffy. Reduce speed and beat in the eggs and vanilla essence, then add raisins (or chocolate and macadamias) and combine well.

Process rolled oats roughly in a blender. Sift flour, baking powder and bicarb soda together and mix together with dry oats. Add this to the wet mixture and mix well.

Place a heaped dessert spoonful of the mixture onto baking trays - keeping approximately 5 cm distance between each as they will spread while baking.

Cook for 10 - 15 minutes depending on how you like your cookies. I cook mine for about 11 minutes as I like a soft chewy cookie. Remove the tray from the oven and let the cookies cool on the tray for about 10 minutes before transferring to a wire rack. Store in an airtight container. These cookies will keep well for 7 - 10 days but they never last that long in my house!

RAISIN COOKIES

Jen's Tip

Use traditional rolled oats. Quick oats give a very different and unusual texture. For perfectly round cookies you can roll these into balls but I like a more rustic look.

Chewy, yummy and full of flavour. These oatmeal and raisin biscuits were a lunch box favourite growing up. I make them with choc chips and macadamia nuts as I have girls who don't like fruit!

Tasty Ginger Biscuits

Prep Time: 15 minutes | Baking Time: 10 - 12 minutes | Makes: 30 small or 16 large

Ingredients

125 g/4 oz butter, softened
2 tablespoons golden syrup
180 g/6 oz sugar
1 beaten egg
300 g/10 ounces self-raising flour
½ teaspoon salt
2 teaspoons ground ginger
White choc discs to top

Method

Preheat your oven to 160° C/320°F (fan forced) and grease your baking tray, or line with baking paper.

Melt the butter and syrup in a saucepan, then add the sugar and egg and mix well using a wooden spoon.

Lastly add flour, salt and ginger (sifted together) and stir to combine.

Roll heaped teaspoon of mixture into balls and place on baking trays, then flatten with white chocolate discs.

Leave 5 cm between biscuits as they will spread while baking.

Bake for 10 - 12 minutes.

This recipe was from Maisie and is delicious. It has the notation *"Easy"* written in the corner.

Jen's Tip

You can add more ginger if you want a stronger flavour. Less baking time gives a soft chewy texture but if you prefer a crisp biscuit, bake a little longer as desired.

ORANGE CAKE

This cake is gluten and dairy free, not that my mum would have ever considered that a "thing". You could use almond meal but I guess that wasn't readily available so she used whole blanched almonds. This is a bitter orange cake but the syrup adds a nice sweetness, or you could simply sprinkle with icing sugar.

Syrup Soaked Orange Cake

Prep Time: 20 - 30 minutes | Baking Time: 60 minutes

Ingredients

2 oranges
1 cup hot water
250 g/8.8 oz blanched almonds
1 cup castor sugar
6 eggs
1 teaspoon baking powder

Syrup

½ cup sugar
¼ cup lemon or orange juice
(or a combination of both)
¼ cup water

Method

Preheat oven to 180°C/350°F (fan forced).
Grease a 20 cm/8" cake tin and line the base with baking paper.
Pierce oranges with a knife 3 - 4 times and simmer in water for 20 minutes with lid on.

Drain the oranges and cool.
Place almonds and sugar in a food processor and blitz until fine then remove from the processor.
Place oranges in the food processor to purée.
You purée the whole orange - skin and all!
Add almond mix, and all other ingredients.
Pulse until combined.
Pour mixture into the tin and bake for 60 minutes.
Leave in the tin and when cake has cooled slightly, pour over warm syrup.
Leave in the tin until completely cool and all syrup has been absorbed.
Remove from tin and decorate if desired.

Syrup

Place all ingredients in a saucepan and bring to the boil stirring until sugar is dissolved.
Cool slightly, before pouring over warm cake. The syrup takes a little time to absorb.

ORANGE CAKE

Glazed Orange Slices

Ingredients

1 - 2 oranges
Iced water
2 cups sugar
2 cups water
3 tablespoons orange juice

Method

Fill a large bowl with ice cubes and water.
Cut oranges into thin slices.
Place these into a saucepan of boiling water and boil for 1 minute.
Remove then immediately place in iced water until cooled.
Drain your slices.

Heat the sugar, water and juice in a wide flat pan e.g. a frypan, over low heat. Stir occasionally until sugar is dissolved.

Place the orange slices in a single layer in the syrup and simmer for approximately 45 minutes.
Turn the slices every 10 - 15 minutes.

Remove your slices from the pan and place on a rack to cool.
Use to garnish your cake when completely cold.

Extra glazed slices keep well in the fridge for 3 - 4 weeks.

Jen's Tips

Blood oranges work well also and give a very different, but equally delicious flavour. This cake browns easily, so covering with alfoil halfway through baking helps.

Delightful Powder Puffs

Prep Time: 20 minutes | Baking Time: 13 - 15 minutes | Makes: 30 small or 15 large

Ingredients

2 eggs
½ cup sugar
½ cup corn flour
1 dessert spoon plain flour
¼ teaspoon bicarb soda
½ teaspoon cream of tartar

Filling

1 - 2 cups whipping cream
1 tablespoon caster sugar
½ teaspoon vanilla extract
Icing sugar for dusting

Method

Preheat oven to 180°C/350°F (fan forced) and line your trays with baking paper.

Separate egg yolks. Beat egg whites and sugar on high speed until thick/soft peaks form. Scrape down the bowl as needed. Add yolks and continue to beat on high speed until combined.

Use a spoon to gently fold in sifted flour, bicarb soda and cream of tartar. Be careful not to over mix, as you want to keep the mixture aerated.

Place baking trays in the oven to warm for a few minutes (ensure they are warm but not too hot).

If making small biscuits, drop approximately one large teaspoon size of mixture onto warm tray.

Keep approximately 5 cm distance between each as they spread during cooking.

If making larger biscuits to stack, drop approximately 2 large tablespoons onto warm tray. Keep 5 cm distance.

Bake for 13 - 15 minutes.

These are known throughout my family as Nan's Powder Puffs: Little pillows of delight.

Assembly

Small biscuits: match into pairs before filling.
Whip cream until soft peaks form, then add sugar and vanilla extract. Continue to whip until combined.
Sandwich with whipped cream and dust with sifted icing sugar on both sides.

Larger stack: These can be served as dessert. Stack 3 or more and fill with layers of
whipped cream, lemon curd or coulis. Add some fresh berries - yum yum.

Cover filled puffs and place in refrigerator for 4 - 6 hours before serving to allow to soften.
This is an essential step.

POWDER PUFFS

Jen's Tips

Using 2 dessert spoons to place the mixture on baking trays is the easiest method. I scoop with one then use the second spoon to scrape onto the tray.

Bake for 13 - 15 minutes until golden. Watch them closely as there is a fine line between perfection and burnt! I sit on a stool in front of the oven and keep an eye on them the whole time. Cool slightly, then remove the paper and reuse the tray with new paper for the next batch.

Once cooled, if they have wrinkled and shrunk you have taken them out too soon. A perfectly cooked puff when cooled should be golden brown, retain its dome shape and be crisp to the touch.

They can be baked ahead of time and will store well in airtight containers for 3 - 4 days, or can be frozen for up to 4 weeks. They must be filled 4 - 6 hours before serving to get the best results.

Maisie's Passion Fruit Shortcake

Prep Time: 10 minutes | Baking Time: 30 minutes

Ingredients

250 g (8 oz) self-raising flour
125 g (4 oz) butter
125 g (4 oz) sugar, plus a little extra
1 egg

Icing

1 cup icing sugar
1 ½ tablespoons soft butter
1 large passion fruit

Method

Preheat the oven to 180°C/350°F (fan forced).
Grease well a 23 cm x 28 cm (9" x 12") tin.
Sift the flour, rub in the butter, then add the sugar.

Beat the egg with a fork and add to your mixture to make a rather dry/crumbly consistency. Pack this into the tin. Rough the surface with a fork, then sprinkle with sugar.

Bake for about 30 minutes or until lightly browned. Once this cools, cut your slice in half and fill with the icing.

Icing: cream the butter and work in the icing sugar and enough passion fruit to make a whipped cream consistency.

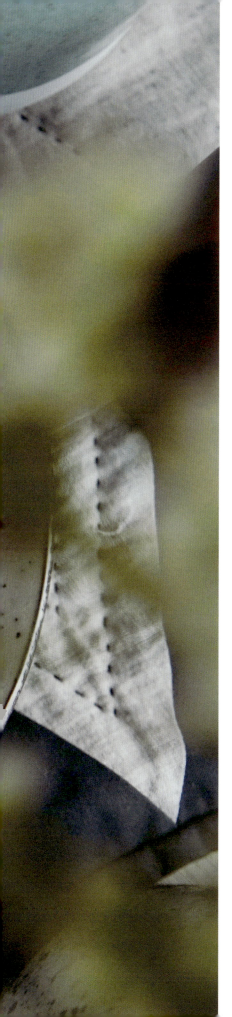

Jen's Tip

I bake mine in a slightly smaller tin and just cut it and drizzle with the passion fruit icing. If I don't have passion fruit I use orange or lemon for the icing.

Jill's Tasty Cupcakes

Prep Time: 10 minutes | Baking Time: 16 - 18 minutes | Makes: 18

Ingredients

2 cups plain flour
1 teaspoon bicarb soda
2 teaspoons cream of tartar
A pinch of salt
1 cup of cream (thickened or whipping)
1 cup of sugar
3 eggs

Method

Preheat your oven to 160°C/320°F (fan forced).

Sift all dry ingredients together.
Place cream in a mixing bowl then add all other ingredients. Beat together for approximately 3 minutes until combined.

Place paper patty pans in a muffin tray to help keep them straight while baking.

Fill each patty pan ⅔ full and place into the oven to bake for 16 - 18 minutes.

Best eaten on the day, but will keep 1 - 2 days in an airtight container.

Ice and decorate as desired.

CUPCAKES

This recipe was given to me by my mother-in-law. It became a staple at every birthday party and a regular lunch box addition. Great for using up cream you might have in the fridge.

Jen with her Mum and Dad at the beginning of her nursing career.

About the Quilter...

Jen Kingwell

Midwife by trade who turned her stitching addiction into a career.

After decades of exploring all areas of the craft world, Jen bought her first patchwork store in 1999. Surrounding herself daily with walls of fabric encouraged her to explore colour combinations and push the boundaries when discovering her signature style, which she describes as "traditional blocks with a modern twist".

It's Jen's use of colour that makes her quilts instantly recognisable. She is a scrap quilter and the more fabrics she can include in any one project the happier she is. Hand stitching is her favourite technique, and teaching all the tips and tricks she knows brings her great joy.

Author, fabric and quilt designer, Jen now travels the world teaching and lecturing but always loves returning to her family and store - Amitié Textiles in Torquay, Australia.

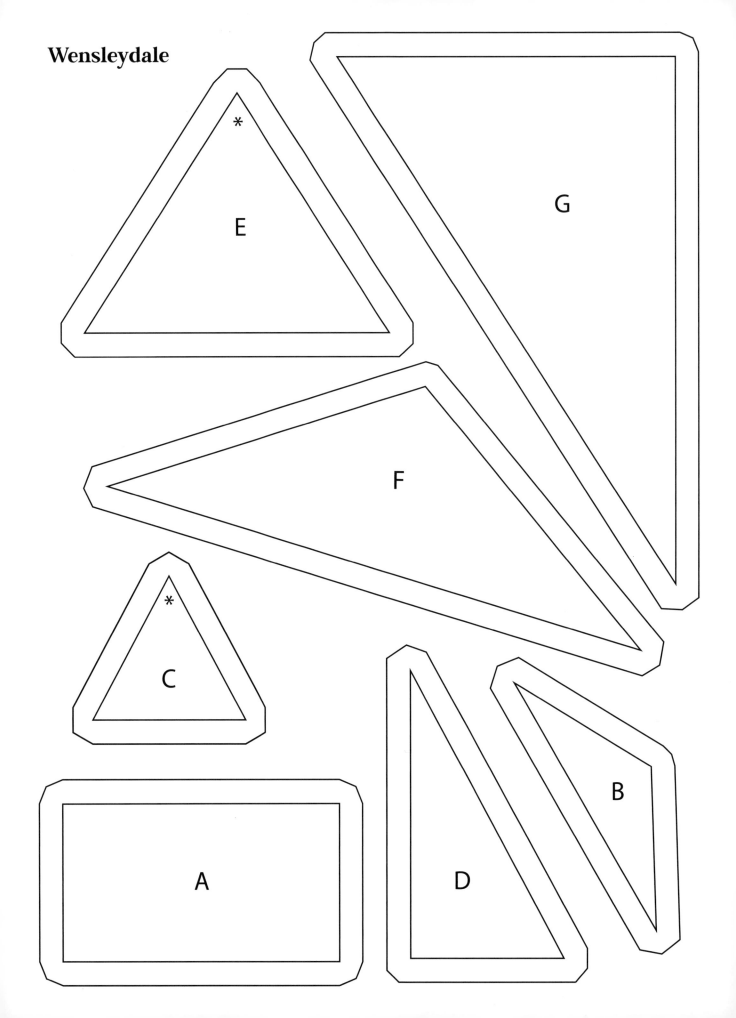

Point Addis

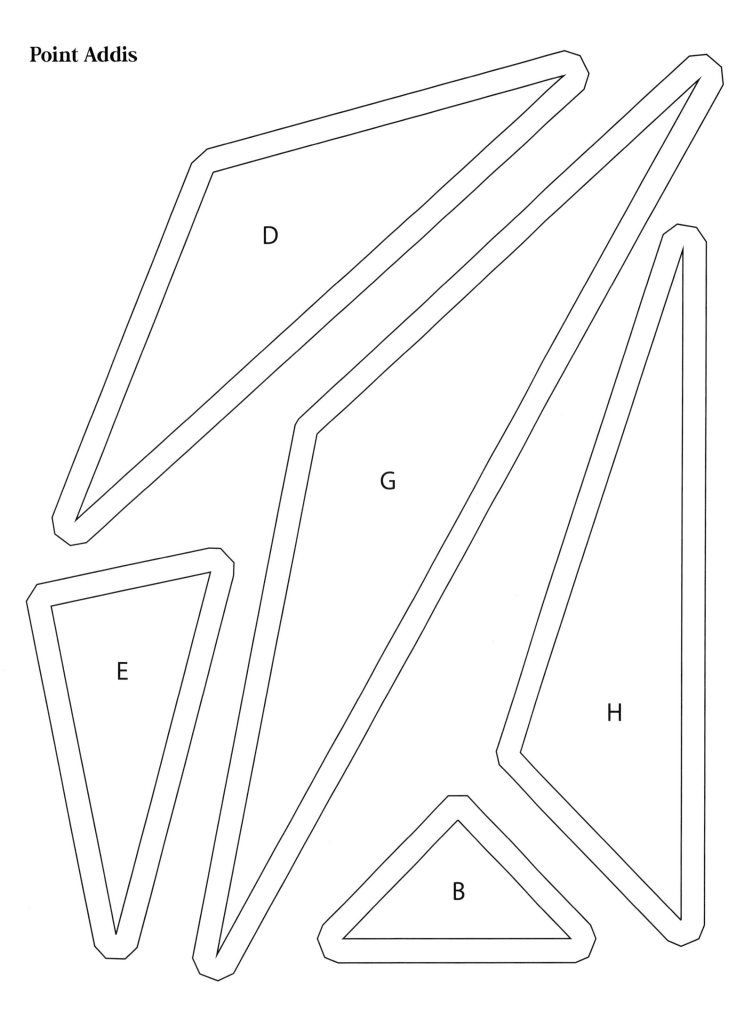

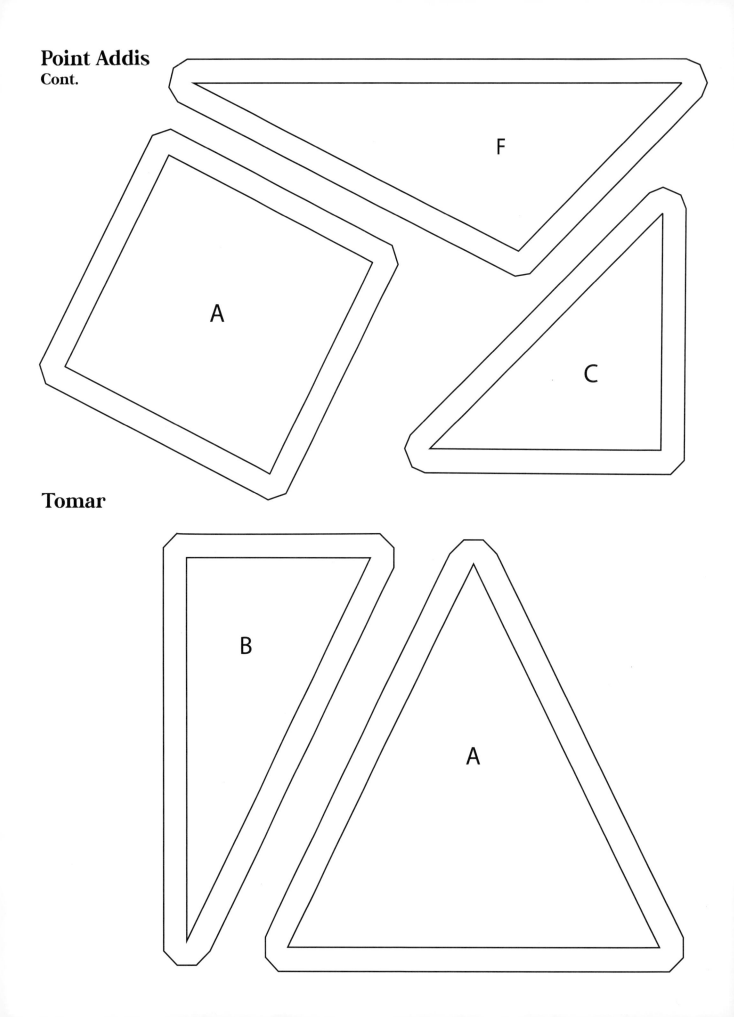

Diamond Exchange

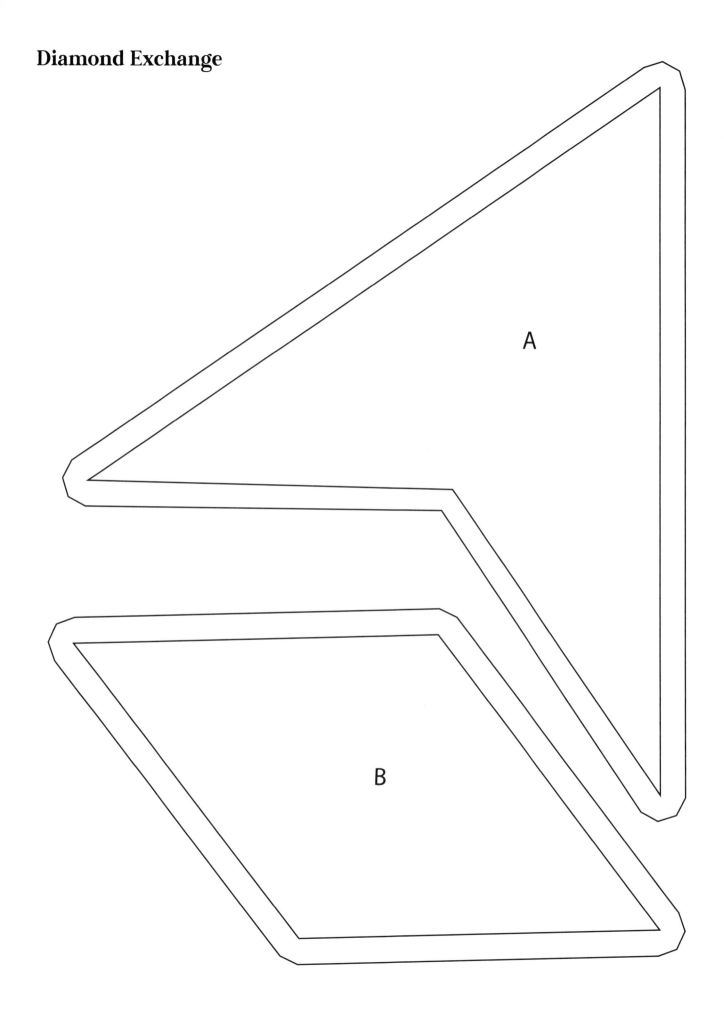

Diamond Exchange

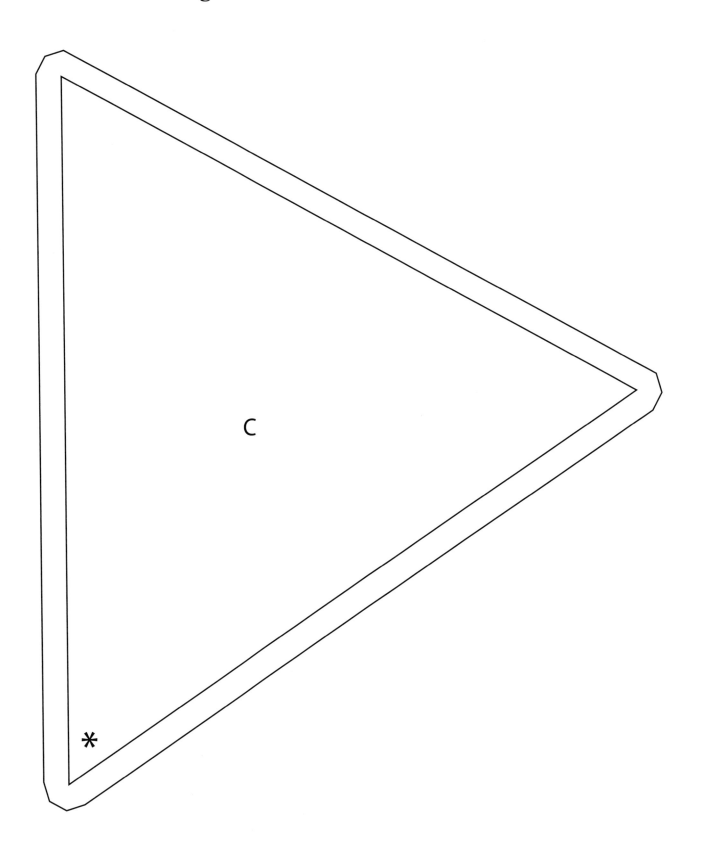

Diamond Exchange

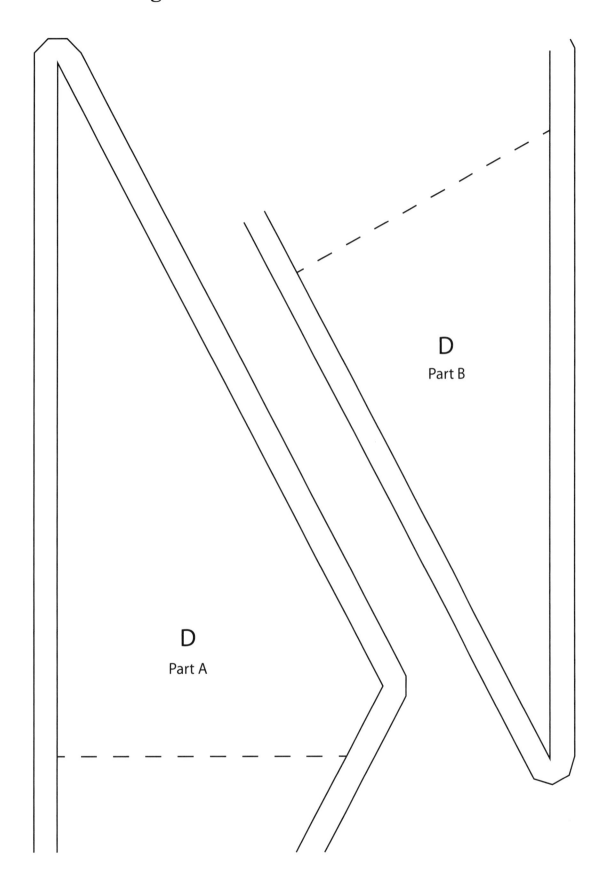

Diamond Exchange
Quilting Guide

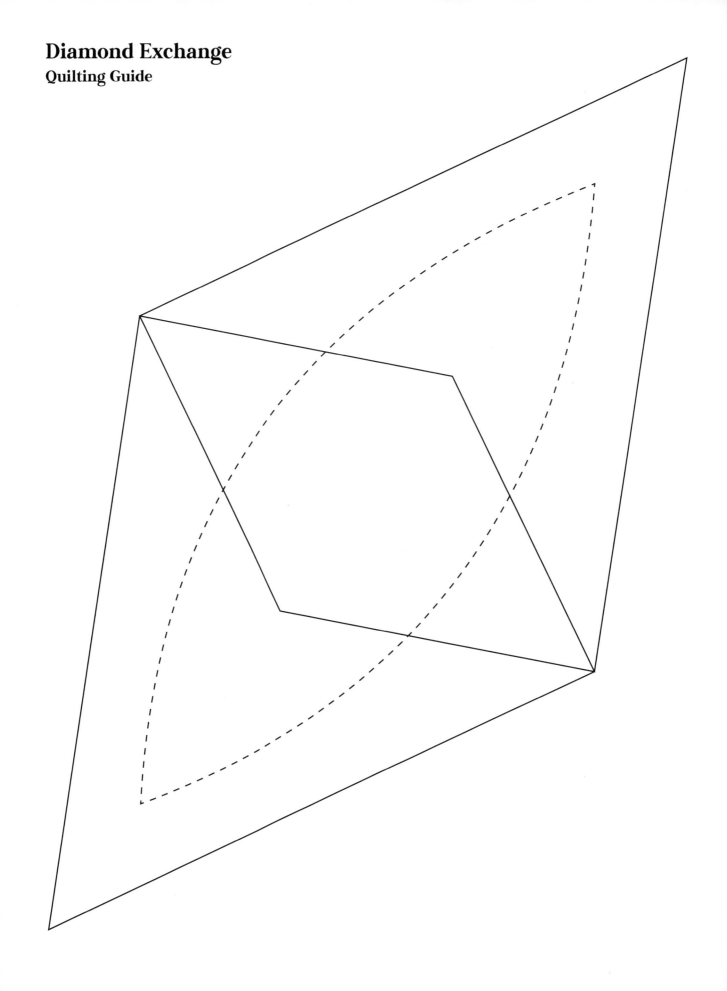

Winki Stars

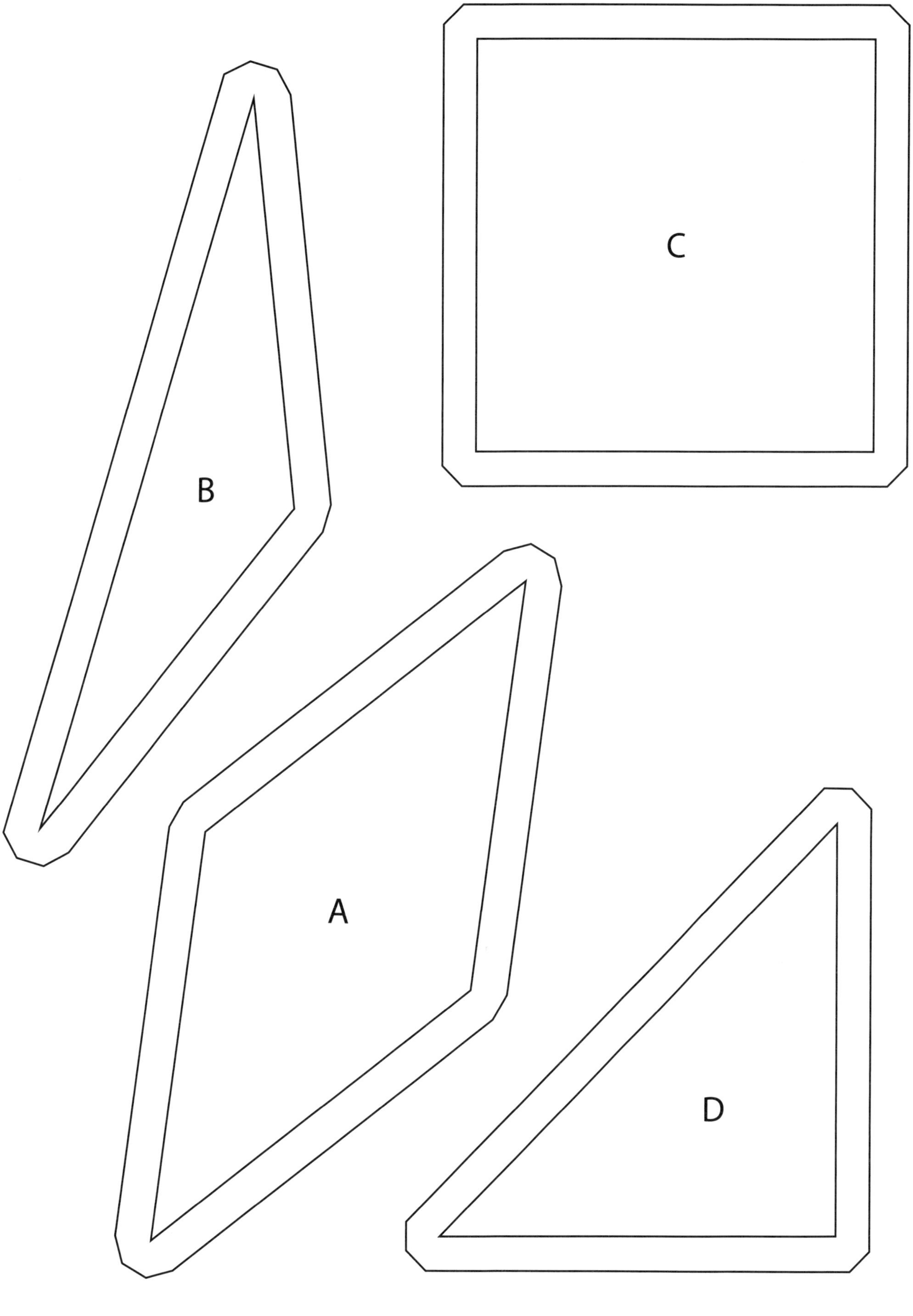

A

B

C

D

Clopin Cushion

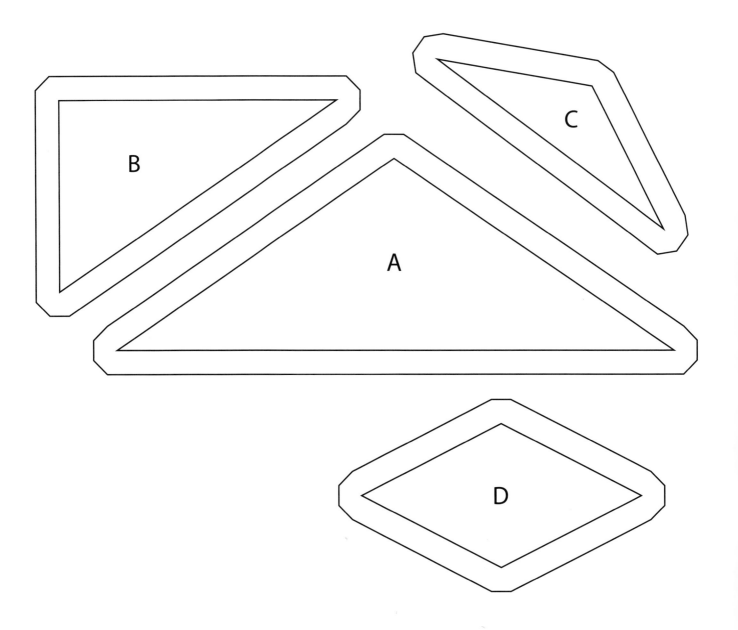

Acknowledgements

Machine Quilting by:

Wendy Gleeson of Clever Ducks Quilting

Lisa Schirmer of Another Quilted Stitch

Photoshoots on location at:

The Wensley, Wensleydale

Room + Board, Daylesford

Some hats supplied by:

Saint Bart

Models:

Caylee Rankin

Michaela Shaw

Olie Birdman

ACKNOWLEDGEMENTS

Creating this book has meant so much to me.
Without your support it wouldn't be possible.
So thank you.

Jen xxx